House

Showing How People Have Lived
Throughout History with Examples Drawn
from the Lives of Legendary Men and Women

By ALBERT LORENZ with JOY SCHLEH

HARRY N. ABRAMS, INC., PUBLISHERS

INTRODUCTION

"House" is one of those words, like "family," that carries a lot of emotional baggage and is sure to evoke a different picture in the mind of each person who uses it. A house, in the everyday sense of the word, is a building where people live, a more or less permanent residence. Often the word is used to mean a single-family dwelling, or, more informally, a comfortable and secure home for Mom, Dad, and the kids. Of course, one has only to say this to see how provincial and small-minded the concept is. What is a family? An Iroquois longhouse of two hundred years ago was a one-family dwelling. The family in this case, however, consisted of all the direct female descendants of the oldest woman, along with their respective husbands and unmarried children. Not what you would expect to find in today's suburban ranch house—but then most people in history would be shocked to see the way we live now.

In this book, the word "house" is used in the broadest possible way: a house is any structure built by human beings to live in for a time. This meaning embraces traditional houses but offers far more than that, seeking to convey some flavor of the amazing diversity of human culture across time and space. Here are houses that people live in as they travel vast distances; houses to segregate groups from the larger society; houses to inspire awe and allegiance; houses built for comfort; houses that express the most refined aesthetic ideals; houses that afford the thinnest margin of survival in a hostile environment.

From a 4,500-year-old Egyptian pyramid, with its secret chambers filled with furnishings and provisions for the dead, to the Mir space station, with its primitive life-support systems, circling the Earth more than 200 miles above our heads, the house is an articulation in three dimensions of every human hope and fear.

The Great Pyramid (far right), the largest surviving pyramid in the world, was built by the pharaoh Khufu.

This pyramid contains two burial chambers inside the structure and one unfinished one beneath it. These burial chambers were plundered long ago, perhaps even before the scene portrayed here.

Many artists, writers, and moviemakers have tried to imagine how the Trojan horse might have looked. This version is rather large, measuring more than forty feet from the top of the head to the ground—roughly equivalent to a three-story building.

SCULPTOR'S HOUSE

The house—a shelter from the elements—is a human necessity. But the house is more than an enclosed space where people conduct their lives: it is also a home for the spirit and it can be a work of art. The ancient Egyptians built houses for the dead that were more durable than those for the living. In fact, they invented the necropolis, a veritable city of the dead. Each tomb in the necropolis was carefully outfitted with the funerary equipment that would ensure its inhabitants a happy afterlife, including statuary, furniture, and wall paintings and texts. A pharaoh might build himself a pyramid, a skyscraper of a tomb, while his courtiers rated small funerary chapels over their burial pits. A whole world of architects, builders, artists, artisans, and laborers was kept busy constructing and maintaining these necropolises.

This is the workshop of a sculptor of funerary statues during the reign of the pharoah Ramses II (1279–1213 B.C.). In the distance is the necropolis of Giza, with its three imposing pyramids and the Sphinx, all built more than a millennium earlier, in a span of about one hundred years (c. 2600–2500 B.C.). The workshop is producing statuettes of cats to accompany departed souls into the afterlife. Cats were a much-loved pet in ancient Egypt and a symbol of the sun-god Ra and his daughter Bastet, the cat-goddess, Like the pyramids, the statuette that the master sculptor is just finishing will survive into the present day, at least in the pages of this book. Don't forget to look for it.

Sculpted House Heroic legends tell of the destruction of the city of Troy in Asia Minor about 1200 B.C. by a Greek army that had besieged the city for nine years. As everyone knows, the Greeks pretended to retreat from the field, leaving behind a large wooden horse as an offering to the goddess Athena. Unbeknownst to the Trojans, the hollow figure housed a squad of Greek soldiers. The Trojans dragged the horse into their city as a token of their great victory. Under the cover of night, the Greek soldiers emerged and opened the city's gates to the rest of the army, which had hidden nearby.

Before turning to the many kinds of historical habitations featured in the pages of this book, it is worth reflecting upon the meaning of the Trojan horse, that troop carrier for a few warriors on a secret mission into enemy territory. The wooden horse is famous in history as an example of a clever trick, but it's a trick that only worked because the Greeks created something that had enormous symbolic value to the Trojans. The city they could not breach by force of arms, they conquered almost overnight by turning a temporary dwelling into a magical work of art.

Many Roman houses had small shrines to household gods. These were the focus of traditional family customs.

Before the Industrial Revolution, it was far more common for houses to incorporate workplaces than today. Many people worked in the same rooms they lived in. Craftsmen often had their own workshops attached to their homes.

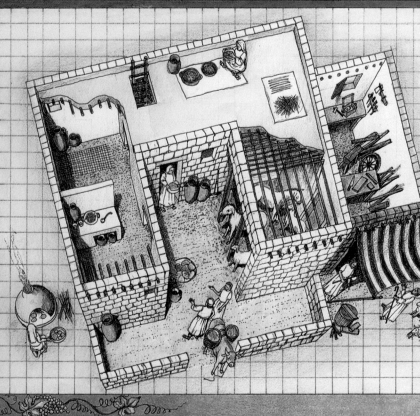

Throughout most of history, only the wealthy could afford houses with specialized rooms, like this library of scrolls.

IMPERIAL GRANDEUR

With a population close to a million people, Rome was the largest city in the world at the turn of the millennium—a metropolis of stone, marble, and concrete. For hundreds of years, imperial officials carried Roman ideas to the far corners of the empire, influencing local customs wherever they went. Here, Pontius Pilate departs from his Roman town house in A.D. 26 to assume the governorship of Judaea, where he was to have the fateful confrontation with Jesus that ended with the Crucifixion some years later.

Even today, particularly in the lands around the Mediterranean and in Latin America, many houses echo the Roman plan, with rooms around the perimeter that open onto a central courtyard or patio. Simply put, the Roman town house created vast amounts of space enclosed by walls. Often surrounded by columned arcades, the house's atriums (large rooms with open skylights), patios, and courtyards were grand but also gaudy spaces, thanks to the heavy use of painted sculpture and ornament. Yet the rooms, for sleeping and reading, cooking and dressing, tended to be small and crowded with family and slaves. Like Roman life in general, the villa glorified power, prestige, and achievement in the public realm. Its use of space placed little value on the intimate daily routines of family life.

Modest Beginnings A Roman patrician like Pontius Pilate was not likely to understand the intense religiosity of the small towns in Judaea and the surrounding lands. When Pilate assumed his post, Jesus was probably living in Nazareth in the house of his parents. Nazareth was a village of about 1,600 people, mostly peasant farmers and craftsmen who also grew some of their own food and kept domestic animals. Houses there would have been constructed of sun-dried or kiln-fired mud bricks, or possibly of dressed stone, with stone or dirt floors and roofs composed of beams packed with earth and branches. Jesus and his father, Joseph, were woodworkers, and their workshop would have been attached to the house, along with a manger for the family's animals. The religious and cultural center of village life was the synagogue.

As in many peasant societies, people in the community shared tasks such as pressing olives and baking bread. For millennia, olives and wheat have been food staples in Mediterranean lands.

SOUTHERN EXPLORATIONS

The presence of human civilizations in remote corners of the world can only be explained by extraordinary feats of exploration and colonization. When people migrate great distances over water, their vessels become temporary homes, for there are no campsites in the ocean. By about A.D. 1000, Asian peoples had settled on islands in the Pacific Ocean that were spread out over an area twice the size of the continental United States. These dauntless travelers appear to have come out of the East about 1500 B.C., mastering the ocean in large sailing canoes.

Another remarkable saga unfolded about A.D. 1100, when groups of South American Indians set out in the Pacific in flotillas of rafts and the Humboldt Current carried them westward. Each raft was probably built of balsa logs and hemp rope. A bamboo cabin roofed with banana leaves would give adequate protection in these mild seas. On journeys that might easily last a hundred days, the voyagers must have survived on rainwater, fish, sweet potatoes, gourds, and coconuts. The more fortunate would have fetched up on the many islands that dot the South Pacific.

Plants like the sweet potato, found today in Polynesia, were probably brought from South America.

Polynesian art seems to have been influenced by Pre-Columbian art from South America.

North America

South America

Humboldt Current

South Pacific Islands

The famous Norwegian anthropologist and explorer Thor Heyerdahl (b. 1914) built a raft called *Kon-Tiki* to prove that voyages like the one described at right were possible. In 1947, his crew traveled for 101 days and 4,300 nautical miles (the distance from Chicago to Moscow) from the west coast of South America to a landfall not far from Tahiti.

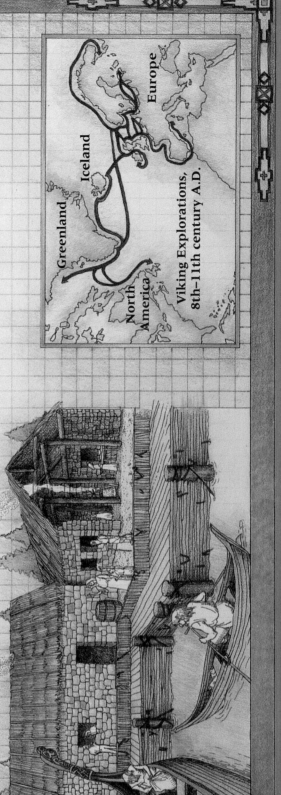

Greenland
Iceland
Europe
North America

Viking Explorations,
8th–11th century A.D.

Northern Explorations

About the time that South American Indians were venturing westward in the Pacific, the Vikings were sending expeditions into the North Atlantic from their villages in Scandinavia. From the eighth to the eleventh century A.D. the Vikings dominated northern Europe. Intrepid colonizers, the Vikings reached Iceland about 870, remote Greenland about 985, and North America in the following decades. As distances between landfalls in the Atlantic were far shorter than in the Pacific, the Vikings did not have to make homes on their vessels, instead establishing farming settlements en route. They built their sturdy farm-houses out of stone, wood, or turf to withstand heavy coastal weather. Like the longhouses of the Iroquois, these were simply "halls" where the family slept, ate, and cooked.

Medieval monasteries were designed to provide for the communal needs of the monks and to separate them from the laymen whose services were required for various practical purposes. At the heart of the building complex was the cloister, an open yard that was surrounded by covered galleries and off-limits to all laymen. (In the overall view on the opposite page, the cloister is tucked between the church and the lower monastic buildings adjacent to it.) In many monasteries, the monks lived in communal dormitories, but often, as in Luther's Augustinian order, they had individual cells. In all cases, they shared their meals in the refectory. The monastery's farmlands were not usually within the building complex.

In an igloo, "furniture" in the form of a sleeping platform and table is made of snow. The women carry burning embers and frozen blubber for the whale-oil lamps that provide heat and light. Seal and caribou skins provide waterproofing and warmth.

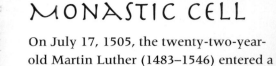

MONASTIC CELL

On July 17, 1505, the twenty-two-year-old Martin Luther (1483–1546) entered a monastery in Erfurt, Germany. The world of the medieval monastery offered a paradox: it was a close-knit community, but it imposed a certain degree of isolation upon its members (in extreme cases, for example, by regulating the times they could speak to one another). In some monastic orders, a monk had pastoral responsibilities in the larger society. In most, however, he simply strove to remain holy while performing the everyday chores necessary for the monastery's survival, and his day was strictly divided among religious observance, work, and reading. In either case, he spent a great deal of time alone, in prayer and contemplation. Within the calm and orderly world of the monastery, medieval monks delved into the world of ideas, and Luther came at the end of a long tradition of monastic scholars. He quickly rose in the hierarchy of his order: in addition being a professor of theology, he soon had responsibility for monasteries scattered throughout his district, as pastor, judge, accountant, and educator. His most important experiences, however, were spiritual ones that were nurtured by solitary study and reflection. It was these epiphanies that gave him the strength to challenge the medieval Church and lead the Protestant Reformation, one of the world's great movements for spiritual renewal.

SNOW HOUSE Isolation may be spiritual or social, but it can also be a sheer physical fact of life. The Eskimo of North America have always been a small population spread over a vast geographic area, most of it the frozen, treeless tundra of the Arctic. During the 5,000-year span that Eskimo have been in North America, they have used many different types of dwellings, some more permanent than others. The most well known is the igloo, a snow house used by Eskimo families in the central Arctic as a temporary shelter during winter seal hunts. The igloo is a perfect house for nomads traveling in small groups over polar ice—one can be erected out of frozen snow in a little more than an hour and will last for weeks. A technological marvel, the igloo is the perfect ecological structure as well: it begins as water and ends as water, leaving no trace on the landscape beyond what is left behind by its inhabitants.

The Eskimo are enormously resourceful about using every part of the animals they hunt. Skins are especially useful in the frozen north.

The queen did not dress herself. The job fell to her ladies in waiting, who coveted the privilege.

Elizabeth was given a commode. Typically, a room with straw on the floor was used as a bathroom.

could have deadly consequences. Elizabeth ordered the execution of her cousin, Mary, Queen of Scots, for plotting against her.

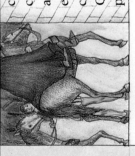

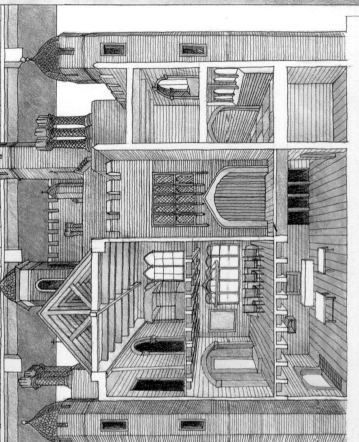

COSTUME DRAMA

The English royal court has probably been responsible for more Hollywood movie epics in which the costumes upstage the story than any other historical phenomenon. We can be forgiven if we think of sixteenth-century England as one enormous pageant starring Queen Elizabeth I (1533–1603) and written by William Shakespeare (1564–1616). Here we see Hampton Court, just outside of London and perhaps the queen's favorite palace, as if it were a stage set for an Elizabethan pageant: although it retains the towers and battlements of the medieval castle, the Renaissance palace is less a fortified refuge than a festive theater for courtly ceremony and political intrigue. The kitchen, as in most grand English houses, is on the lower floor—hence the use of the expression "belowstairs" to refer to the servants. A banquet is about to be served in the throne room above the kitchen. The royal bedroom is on the top floor. Elizabeth was a restless monarch, and the court moved from house to house at her whim, to escape disease, or simply because after being inhabited for a while, a palace would become a filthy mess and need a thorough cleaning. The queen really made the whole nation her dwelling: in the summer she ventured into the countryside (this was called a "progress") with her retinue to stay with members of the local nobility, who dreaded these visits because of the cost of entertaining an army of high-living courtiers.

A Lively Scene William Shakespeare—who, more than anyone else, came to exemplify the values of the Elizabethan age—was born in this house (far left) in 1564, when Elizabeth was thirty-one years old. William's father was a glove maker, and the house included both the family's living quarters and a workshop. Like many Elizabethan buildings, Shakespeare's birthplace, and his Globe Theater in London (left), which burned in 1613, display the highly decorative half-timber construction that was used throughout northern Europe since Roman times, adding another kind of pageantry to city and countryside.

In half-timber construction, a framework is built and then the spaces between the timbers are filled with wattle and daub (woven rods and twigs covered with clay), bricks, and windows. Different regions of northern Europe developed their own characteristic half-timber designs.

Moral lessons were given with a bluntness that would disgust us today. On London Bridge, the heads of traitors and criminals were displayed on spikes for the edification of passersby.

One famous resident of London Bridge was the moral philosopher Desiderius Erasmus (c. 1466–1536), who published a popular book in 1530 called *On Civility in Children*. It included the advice: "Don't be the first to reach into the pot. . . . And don't put your whole hand in it—use only three fingers at most."

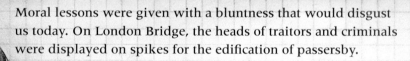

COUNTRY PEOPLE

The end of the Middle Ages in Europe was an exciting time to be alive. You can see it in the art of a painter like Pieter Brueghel (c. 1525–1569), rich in color and action and passion. Here, in a peasant cottage in Flanders in the mid-sixteenth century, an extended family (including three generations and unmarried collateral relations) shares its space with as many useful animals as the household can afford. A midday meal is in progress. Filth and grunge rule, but it's a lusty and vibrant life for the healthy. The hearth with its bubbling stockpot serves both for cooking and for heating, and a good thing too, since there's no glass in the window to keep out the weather. The beaten dirt floor is carpeted with straw, which also floats down from the sleeping loft above. At the end of the day, the table and benches will be moved aside, and people who can't fit in the loft will sleep on the floor. Through the window you can see the small parish church around which this family's little world revolves. In the middle of the picture is a visiting merchant, whose formal dress contrasts with the peasants' simple, loose garb. This family has few possessions beyond farming tools and some cookware, but everyone in medieval Europe was involved in trade in one way or another. Flanders lay across main trade routes between London, Paris, and the Rhine.

City People

The hub of trade is the city, where every inch is densely packed with houses. The Flemish merchant in the scene above trades with an English merchant who works and lives on London Bridge, a major entryway into the city. Unlike the peasant cottage, some of the homes on London Bridge would have had indoor privies, but these emptied directly into the Thames River, making for comic and revolting accidents for hapless boatmen. Not for nothing was it said, "Wise men go over and fools go under."

The Dutch artist Jan Vermeer painted domestic scenes like this one, but never with so many people in them. However, it's important to remember that houses in the past were almost always crowded.

In the crowded holds, chains bound the captives together by arms, legs, and necks. These are the most oppressive living conditions you will see in this book.

DUTCH MASTERS

It appears to be a general rule of life that the comforts enjoyed by the privileged come at a cost, and, furthermore, that often the cost is borne by others. A mid-seventeenth-century Dutch merchant family that profits from the slave trade celebrates the engagement of the eldest son. The groom is showing his nephew a model of one of the family firm's ships, while his betrothed plays the virginals, a small instrument similar to a piano, in the back of the room. Dutch families such as this one practically invented the idea of the comfortable single-family house. Their homes were snug and orderly, with public rooms downstairs and bedrooms upstairs. They preferred chairs with backs to the more traditional benches and stools, and they covered tables with thick rugs, a practice that survives in Holland to this day. Their walls were decorated with paintings and prints, and they proudly displayed maps and globes, symbols of their nation's wealth and power. Dutch women were stereotyped as being fanatical housekeepers, endlessly scrubbing and cleaning. This obsession with cleanliness did not extend to the body, however—the seventeenth-century Dutch were notorious throughout Europe for not bathing.

Slave Ship

Throughout seventeenth-century Europe, merchants' wealth was founded in part on the misery of the slave trade. That innocent ship in the bottle (above) happens to have been the model of a slaver in the notorious "triangle trade." Merchants sailed south from European seaports to the west coast of Africa to buy slaves, transported them to the West Indies to be sold, and filled their holds with sugar and other staples for the return trip to Europe. Slaves were treated as cargo.

Europe

West Indies

Africa

The Triangle Trade

The *Galerie des Glaces,* or Hall of Mirrors, which took eight years to decorate (1678–86) was the palace's main reception room. Thanks to seventeen mirrors along one wall that echo the large windows on the opposite wall, the room would have sparkled with thousands of points of light when all of the twenty chandeliers were lit of an evening. During the king's lifetime, the hall was filled at all hours with jostling crowds of courtiers, ministers, servants, and tourists.

A New England Puritan would have been appalled by Versailles, but that doesn't mean she didn't show off her own valued possessions. Many kitchens had dressers like the one seen at right, on the back wall, where the family's best pewter and ceramic flatware, probably imported from England, was proudly displayed.

Hall of Mirrors

The country house that King Louis XIV (1638–1715) of France built for himself around the nucleus of a favorite hunting lodge of his father's in the village of Versailles, about fifteen miles west of the center of Paris, was to become the most famous royal residence in the world—the standard by which every other splendid dwelling was judged. It was said that there were 10,000 people living on its grounds and 36,000 laborers working on the construction in the 1680s, when the king was in his prime.

For the king, the palace of Versailles, which he made the official seat of government in 1682, was an exquisite instrument of power. His courtiers, all powerful nobles in their own right, desperately wished to be close to his side

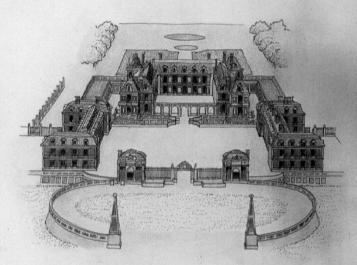

to obtain the favors that only he could provide, and for them Versailles was a gilded prison. When they were there, they were completely at the mercy of the king, who kept them occupied with an elaborate (and costly) regimen of social and ceremonial obligations. These would include mandatory attendance at the king's *lever* (the complex ritual of getting him out of bed in the morning) and *coucher* (bedtime), his midday mass, his dinner, his audiences, and his hunts (after which came the *débotter,* when he changed out of his hunting clothes).

Starter Home In 1686, when the *Galerie des Glaces* was finally complete, Peter Coffin and John Gardner—Puritans of Nantucket Island off Massachusetts—got together to build a house for their newly married children, Jethro

and Mary. In matters of style, the Puritans were the spiritual descendants of Martin Luther: they lived in plain houses and dressed in plain clothing and were generally critical of ostentation and the conspicuous display of wealth.

Viewed in the very broadest perspective, this house and thousands like it scattered across the New England countryside descend directly from the peasant cottage in Flanders, but feature a far more elaborate division into rooms according to function. Cooking has been relegated to the lean-to-like kitchen in the back of the house. The front of the house, which faces south to gather in a maximum amount of light, contains the hall, where the family takes its meals and where some might sleep. Even at this late date, the front door is likely to open into the hall, without a vestibule. There are separate bedchambers downstairs and upstairs.

A corridor ran down the center of the longhouse. It was lined on either side by two-tiered platforms. Each family occupied a section of these platforms, sleeping together on the bottom one on bearskin rugs and keeping their possessions on the upper one. Women cooked indoors on open fires, filling the space with smoke.

Unlike the Iroquois, the Bedouin strictly separate families by gender in their dwellings: each tent is divided by a curtain that separates the men's quarters from the harem, where the women and children sleep and the household work—cooking, weaving—is done.

LONGHOUSE

The five tribes that formed the famous League of the Iroquois in the late sixteenth century first appeared in what is present-day New York State about two hundred years earlier. The warlike league—made up of the Seneca, the Oneida, the Cayuga, the Onondaga, and the Mohawk—came to dominate the rich lands between the Hudson and Niagara rivers, a territory that the Iroquois regarded as a symbolic longhouse sheltering the tribes peaceably together. The longhouse was a long structure constructed of poles lashed together and covered with sheets of bark. Each one was a communal home for more than a dozen families related through a maternal line: female descendants of the oldest woman remained in the house with their families, while male descendants moved into the longhouses of the women they married. An Iroquois village consisted of a cluster of longhouses encircled by a fence but rarely lasted more than twenty years in the same location: as the farmland wore out and the corn crop declined, the village would gradually be moved to an undeveloped site nearby.

Tent

Long before the Iroquois arose in North America, Bedouin tribes roamed the Arabian Desert. Like the Eskimo, the Bedouin inhabit an environment of extremes—in their case, not wet and cold but dry and, in summer, brutally hot. These nomads, who can travel up to forty miles a day on camelback, carry their houses with them in the form of black tents made of goat's hair and wool that can be pitched quickly at night (the word *arab* means "tent dweller"). Traditionally, the Bedouin have been camel breeders, keeping their own herds and often raiding those of other tribes. In summer they camp near water but for nine months of the year they wander the vast desert, pasturing their herds, and rarely staying in one place for more than ten days at a time. The marvelous camel is a veritable recycling system for its human owner: it can drink brackish water unfit for people, and a female with calf can produce a gallon of milk a day for eleven months.

Jefferson loved the polygraph (left), a machine for copying letters. He designed his own labor-saving devices, like a revolving bookstand (below) and a hidden dumbwaiter (right).

In this cabin for a family of Russian serfs, the bed is heated by the hearth, a useful design for a very cold climate.

INGENIOUS EDIFICE

Very few people have the opportunity to design and build their own dream house. Thomas Jefferson (1743–1826), author of the Declaration of Independence and third president of the United States, was one of them. Monticello, in Virginia's Blue Ridge Mountains, was the work of half a lifetime: forty years elapsed between the time he selected the site in 1768 and his return to a (more or less) finished house at the end of his presidency in 1809. The house was a perfect expression of its builder's character and interests, reflecting not only Jefferson's ideas about art and architecture (which were shaped by many years of living in Europe) and his genius for practical innovation, but also his quirks and eccentricities. Jefferson liked to work in bed, and his bed was unusual in that it completely filled a hall between two rooms, so that on one side of it was his bedroom proper and on the other a small study that he called his "cabinet room." In this illustration, the walls are indicated by their outlines: Jefferson is seated on the bed facing into the bedroom; the cabinet room is behind him, on the other side of the bed. If Monticello is a dream, so too, in a way, is this portrayal of it, for gathered here are the youthful spirits of some of the signers of the Declaration of Independence, visiting Jefferson in his house. Jefferson died in this bed on the Fourth of July, 1826.

This revolving door with shelves on the back is typical of Jefferson's designs.

These are the rooms at left, seen from the other side.

Palace of Thought

Palace of Thought The eighteenth century produced many enlightened leaders, who, like Jefferson, loved the arts as much as the art of politics. One was Empress Catherine the Great (1729–1796) of Russia, who lived in the grand palaces of Saint Petersburg reading, and corresponding with, the most advanced philosophers of the day (like Jefferson, she often worked in her bedroom). The French philosopher Voltaire (1694–1778, left) influenced the political thinking of both leaders. Like Erasmus, whom we met earlier in this book, he had a skeptical view of the morals of the rich and powerful. Catherine corresponded with Voltaire, and Jefferson displayed his portrait bust in the Entrance Hall at Monticello. Curiously, in spite of their ideals, neither the empress nor the president sought to put an end to the system of slavery (in Russia, it was called serfdom) in their respective societies.

The parlor floor of Holmes's house is crammed with the furnishings and objects that are mentioned in his adventures, and also sports the "V. R." (for Victoria Regina) written in bullet holes on the parlor wall, a patriotic salute to the queen executed by

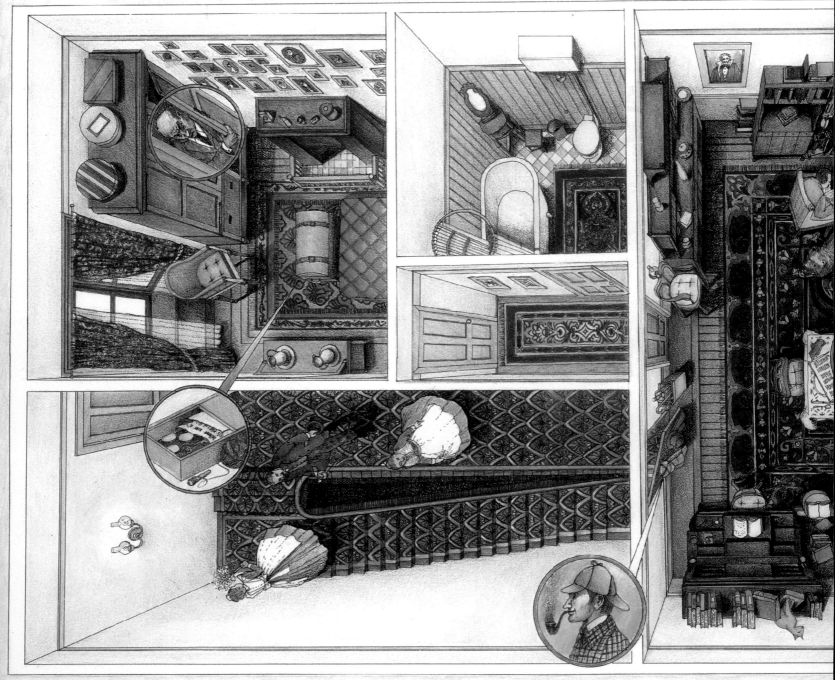

Holmes with a "hair-trigger" revolver in the story "The Musgrave Ritual." Hiding in the wardrobe in Holmes's bedroom, with its wall of pictures of famous criminals, is his nemesis, the evil Professor Moriarty.

In the Zulu huts, furnishings were largely limited to grass sleeping mats with carved wooden headrests; a fire in the chimneyless space ensured that it would be warm but smoky.

BACHELORS' LAIR

This is a view of the parlor floor of 221B Baker Street, London, in the 1880s. At this fictional address, two famous bachelors lived together, at least until one got married: they were the great detective Sherlock Holmes (playing his violin by the window) and his able chronicler Dr. John Watson (seated by the fireplace). The small city row house is a direct descendant of our Dutch town house, although enormous technological progress has been made in the three hundred years that separate them. For example, indoor plumbing has come into its own in this house, and at least the main rooms are lit by gas lamps. Coal is used for cooking and heating.

The typical Victorian household employed rather more help than most people can afford nowadays. In the hall, you can see the estimable landlady Mrs. Hudson trailed by a maid wielding a feather duster. Armies of women labored on behalf of middle-class families in the nineteenth century, caring for children, cooking, cleaning, washing, and performing a innumerable other tasks. And thanks to vastly increased production of domestic furnishings, there was a lot more to take care of, an outpouring of goods—many machinemade—that threatened to overrun every available surface.

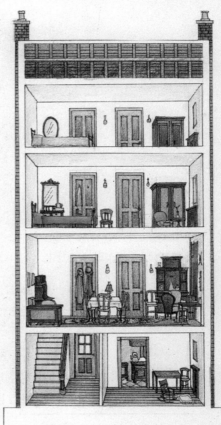

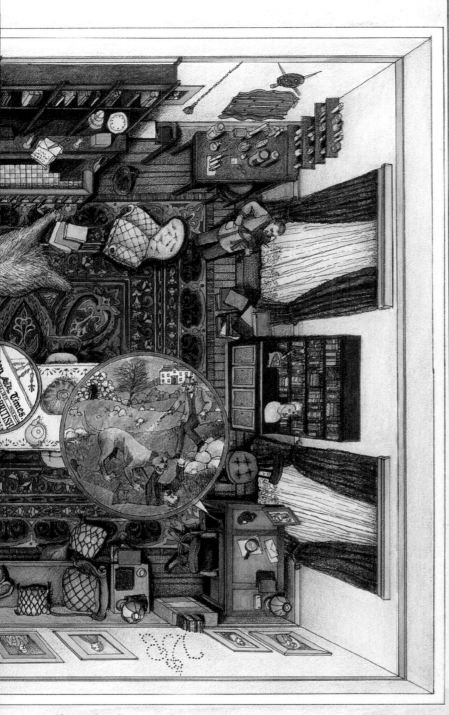

Readers of Holmes's adventures will recognize the cameo commemorating a dramatic moment in "The Hound of the Baskervilles."

Warrior's Corral

An old copy of the *London Times* on Holmes's parlor table announces the defeat in 1879 of a British army by warriors of the Zulu kingdom (located in what is now the province of Natal in the Republic of South Africa). The Zulu lived in homesteads consisting of a man and his three or four wives, each with his or her own hut made of woven saplings covered with grass thatch. These huts were arranged in a circle around a pen for cattle, which measured a man's wealth and status as well as fed the group (the Zulu, like Brueghel's peasants, subsisted partly on milk curds). Virtually every male Zulu served the king as a warrior for a span of fifteen to twenty years, when he could expect to spend as much as half his time away from his homestead. A royal homestead hosting the sovereign's regiments became a veritable city of huts.

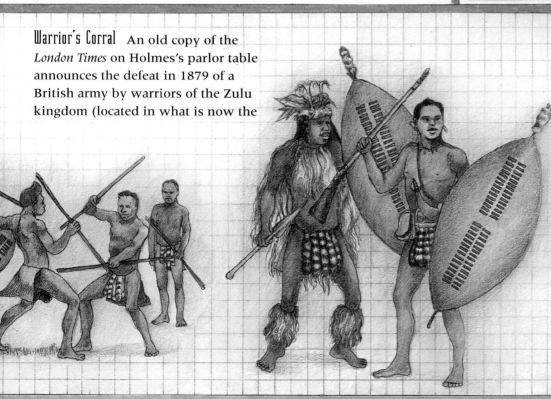

FLOATING FACTORY

The golden age of the New England whale fishery lasted roughly thirty years, from the 1830s to the Civil War. The New England whaler was both factory and barracks, a world of men working and living together under one roof. (Only the captain had the privilege of bringing his wife on a voyage, and when he did—as is the case here—his ship was known as a "hen frigate.") This was a hierarchical society in a small space: the captain's cabin was in the stern of the vessel; officers had their own staterooms, not far from the captain's; sailors bunked together in the bow.

As whaling voyages could be measured in months and, sometimes, even years, it was imperative that the crew possess all of the skills necessary to keep a ship in business. In addition to sailors (who were also versed in the arts of hunting whales and harvesting oil and bone), crews included blacksmiths and coopers, carpenters and cooks. The ship carried most of its own provisions, including fresh water. The hold was filled with casks, which contained various necessities on the outward voyage and would be filled with whale oil for the return. Thus, the whaler was an example of a closed structure for housing human beings equipped with its own "life-support systems." In this regard, it presaged the space stations of today.

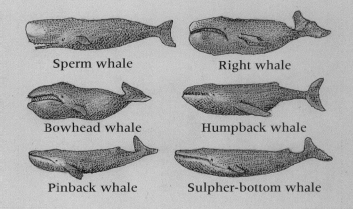

Sperm whale   Right whale

Bowhead whale   Humpback whale

Pinback whale   Sulpher-bottom whale

Houseboat

Around the world, from Seattle to Amsterdam to Hong Kong, hundreds of thousands of people live on boats. Houseboats range in design from simple floating platforms that are rarely, if ever, moved to mothballed vessels that are adapted to the needs of domestic life. Occasionally, workboats double as family homes—this is not practical on the high seas, but a vessel that plies rivers and canals on regular routes need not separate a husband from his wife and children. It is not uncommon in Chinese ports for families to live together on junks that come and go on local trading cruises. The junk itself is an amazingly sturdy and versatile vessel, with high walls that are easily adaptable to living quarters and watertight compartments that make them especially seaworthy.

Exhilarated by his work on the house, Church wrote, "I can make more and better landscapes in this way than by tampering with canvas and paint in the Studio."

HOUSE AND GARDEN

In 1883, when the French Impressionist painter Claude Monet (1840–1926) was looking for a house for his large family, he settled on a two-acre property in the village of Giverny, forty miles northwest of Paris. After about a decade of painting the surrounding countryside, Monet began to focus his attention on the beautiful gardens the family had cultivated. He spent months dickering with the village to obtain the permits he needed to dredge a pond, and there he installed a garden of water lilies, along with a small Japanese-style footbridge, the subject of a memorable series of paintings dating from the turn of the century (right cameo). Soon Monet's imagination because fixed on the lily pond. It was to become the subject of some of the last great paintings of his life (left cameo), vast canvases that portray its shimmering surface. In 1915 he built a large studio (top right), with rolling easels that could hold canvases six by twelve feet. He was seventy-five years old and his vision was beginning to falter, but he persevered.

Visitors found the house, grounds, and studio filled with paintings of the garden (one described a row of easels lined up and holding a series of unfinished canvases waiting for the artist to catch the changing light). The property became for Monet all the world he needed to pursue his art.

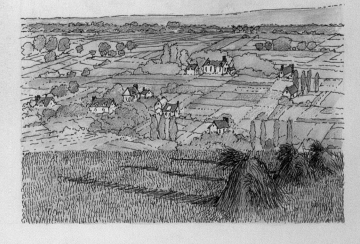

Room with a View A bit more than ten years before Monet found Giverny, the American landscape painter Frederic E. Church (1826–1900) built a house about one hundred miles north of New York City on a ridge overlooking the Hudson River. Church designed the ornamental details using motifs from Persian architecture (opposite), and his wife named the place Olana, a probable corruption of the Arabic "Al'ana," for "our place on high." On high it was, with a spectacular view of the river and the green landscape stretching westward, a vista that Church had painted many times in his life. By placing a house that was an exotic fantasy (Church had never actually been to Persia) in a landscape that was intensely familiar, the artist satisfied two seemingly conflicting artistic needs. Monet and Church lived in their houses until their deaths in, respectively, 1926 and 1900. There is no record that they ever visited one another.

Monet and Church both created settings where they could pursue their art. Monet was, in the end, drawn to garden subjects close at hand. Church responded to distant vistas, particularly the spectacle of the setting sun over the Hudson River, which was visible from his studio window.

In the prisons of Devil's Island, as in every other human habitation, all of the varieties of human behavior flowered, ranging from the compassionate treatment of tropical diseases by convict nurses to brutal floggings to a thriving black market in goods and services. A prisoner who survived his sentence would live out his days in Guiana, as most were not permitted to return to France. Few were informed of this regulation at the time of sentencing.

As soon as there were long-distance railroad routes, there were designs for railroad cars with luxurious accommodations for wealthy travelers, including sleeping cabins, dining cars, and lounges, providing all the comforts of a gracious home.

Uniforms did little to stifle self-expression. Prisoners decorated their bodies with elaborate tattoos.

TROPICAL PRISON

Since the seventeenth century, millions of Europeans have left their homelands to make new lives. Of these, a fair portion departed in disgrace, dispatched by criminal (and political) courts to far-off penal colonies where, out of sight, they would presumably rot away. Early on, the English sent debtors to Georgia and criminals to Australia. For a hundred and fifty years up until World War II, the French sent convicted criminals to French Guiana, on the northeast coast of South America. Here were the isolated labor camps collectively called "Devil's Island," after a small island off the coast where political prisoners were held. Most transportees were lightly guarded, since, as new arrivals were told, "the real guards here are the jungle and the sea." But those who were considered particularly dangerous were kept in more traditional prisons, where they were isolated in Spartan cells, garbed in red and white striped uniforms, and put to work under conditions of military discipline. Incorrigible prisoners were sent to the guillotine.

Hotel on Wheels The twice-yearly steamship to Devil's Island carried iron cages that each held ninety men. A happier means of leaving Europe in the interwar years was the Venice Simplon Orient Express between Paris and Istanbul (Simplon was the name of the twelve-mile tunnel through the Alps, completed in 1906, that made the route much more direct). The coaches built for the Orient Express in the 1920s were the world's finest, and the fifty-six hour journey from the heart of one continent to the edge of another was a glamorous experience that provided unparalleled opportunities for romance and intrigue.

The lowest temperature recorded on Earth was -89.2°C (-128.6°F), at Vostok Station in Antarctica, on July 21, 1983. Today, there are settlements in Antarctica. These would have been inconceivable in Shackleton's day. No one, however, can devise housing that is very comfortable in such extreme weather conditions.

INN DOWN UNDER

Wherever there are travelers, there are establishments to house them: hotels, motels, inns, taverns, and a hundred local variations. At the very least, they provide the weary with a room and a meal, but they are also windows onto the outside world for towns and villages that would otherwise be islands unto themselves. This turn-of-the-century inn in the Australian town of Cowra has attracted a festive crowd on a Saturday night. The location is reminiscent of the American frontier: westward from this inn lies an awesome expanse of flat, arid terrain that is largely undeveloped save for ranches and scattered mines and oil wells, but home to aboriginal peoples and such quintessentially Australian critters as the kangaroo, the koala, and the platypus.

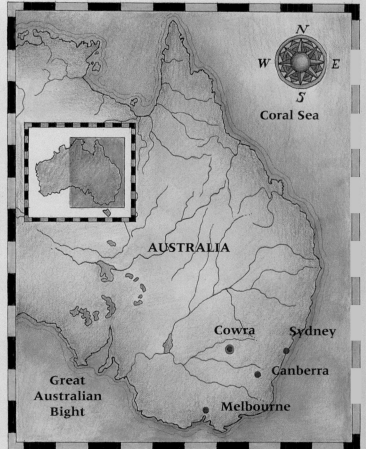

ENDURANCE The last frontier for intrepid European explorers was Antarctica, the only continent without an indigenous human population. In 1914, the Irish explorer Ernest Shackleton (1874–1922) launched an ill-fated expedition to cross the inhospitable landmass. His ship, the *Endurance*, was immobilized by ice in January 1915 and crushed the following November; twenty-eight men were left to battle their way back to safety. For five months, they drifted north on an ice floe, until the pack ice broke up enough for them to launch their boats and make for Elephant Island, eight hundred miles from the nearest inhabited island. Shackleton struck out for help in the biggest boat, leaving twenty-two men behind. All were eventually rescued, a year and a half after the *Endurance* was first trapped. For four and a half months on Elephant Island, the ragged expedition lived in a hut formed from one of the upturned boats; two surgeons even managed to amputate one man's frostbitten toes successfully in a jerry-built "operating room." Survival in these conditions was a testament to leadership, cooperation, and self-discipline.

There are no land-based vertebrate animals in Antarctica. Penguins are the most commonly encountered inhabitants.

Gaudí created a vocabulary of architectural forms that were inspired by nature. His tiles resembled a reptile's skin, his spires looked like exotic plants, his balconies were reminiscent of animal skulls.

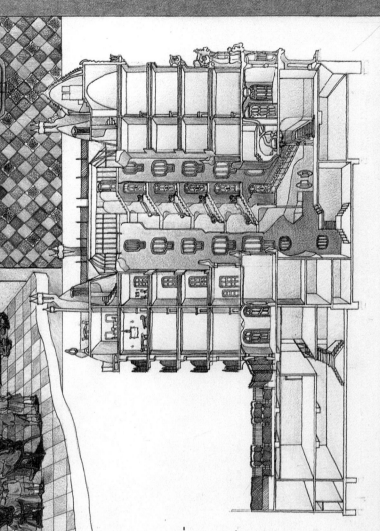

ARTFUL APARTMENT HOUSE

In the first decades of the twentieth century, architects began to think in original ways about the housing needs of the urban middle classes, which often meant designing apartment buildings rather than private homes. Antoni Gaudí (1852–1926), who was one of the most imaginative talents of the past two hundred years, built the Casa Batlló (1905–7) in his hometown of Barcelona. This small gem had, as one writer put it, "interiors which seem to have been hollowed out by the waves of the sea," an appropriate image for a building in Spain's major seaport. A popular interpretation of the building holds that it symbolizes Saint George slaying the dragon: the tower crowned with a cross represents the saint's lance thrust into the body of the dragon, and the bonelike stone ornaments on the second floor windows (seen in the cameo top right) are the remains of the dragon's victims. The fanciful structures on the roof are part of the dragon's spine. Whatever the architecture might symbolize, in practical terms the building had to provide a comfortable setting for the lives of Barcelona's bourgeois citizens. In this sense, it was not so different from the Victorian row house where Holmes and Dr. Watson lived. It was simply many row houses stacked one upon the other.

Life in a Trench

In the summer of 1914 the most destructive war in history erupted across Europe. For tens of thousands of soldiers, home for the next four years would be the trench, a grotesque variation on the apartment house. Essentially a fortified bunker dug into the earth and stretching for hundreds of miles, with rudimentary accommodations for soldiers, the trench was a way for an army to hold its position. The opposing army would bombard the trench with artillery shells, rarely scoring a direct hit. A man might pass a lifetime in the Casa Batlló, but few could endure more than a week at a time under enemy fire in the trenches.

MUSICAL MECCA

Harlem, near the northern end of Manhattan Island, was the most important center of black cultural life in America beginning in the 1920s. A vibrant city within a city, it attracted musicians, artists, and writers seeking inspiration and community, not to mention fame and fortune. Jazz was the popular art form of Harlem. New York was one of a handful of cities that offered the aspiring jazz musician room to grow—not only a place to live, but places to play, an audience to play to, and other musicians to play with. Oddly enough, the apartment building played a role in creating a New York jazz tradition. For one thing, apartment buildings often have mixed commercial and residential uses, and in Harlem they were home to many nightclubs—ranging from big, fancy establishments that attracted people from all over the city to small clubs for locals only—where musicians earned their keep. A less obvious factor was the Harlem tradition of the rent party. Tenants would hold parties, invite jazz and blues musicians to play, and charge a modest admission to raise money to pay the rent. Between the rent parties and the nightclubs, there was music in the air every night.

1. Johnny Dodds (1892–1940), clarinetist from New Orleans, Louisiana.
2. Lil Hardin (1898–1971), pianist from Memphis, Tennessee.
3. Duke Ellington (1899–1974), bandleader and composer, from Washington, D.C.
4. Bessie Smith (c. 1894–1937), blues singer, from Chattanooga, Tennessee.
5. Clyde Bernhardt (1905–1986), trombonist from Gold Hill, North Carolina.
6. Coleman Hawkins (1904–1969), tenor saxophonist, from St. Joseph, Missouri.
7. Louis Armstrong (1901–1971), trumpet player, bandleader, and singer from New Orleans, Louisiana.

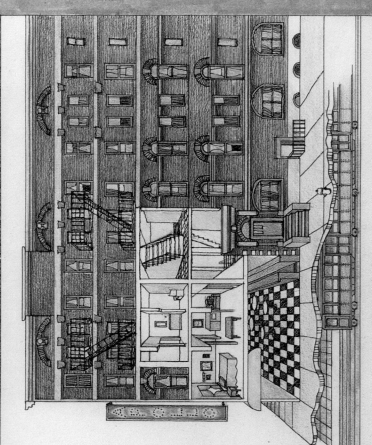

Southern Roots

Often, an art form begins in a traditional culture and is carried to cosmopolitan cities where it evolves quickly under the pressure of innovation. Such was the case with jazz and blues. Many of the great African-American musicians of the 1920s and 1930s came from the South, not only from cities like New Orleans, Louisiana, but also rural villages where music and music making had been an important part of everyday family life for generations. Music permeated religious worship, celebrations and holidays, and even certain kinds of work, particularly farming.

Jazz returned to the places where it began via the portable record player and the radio, which filled houses everywhere with music in the twentieth century.

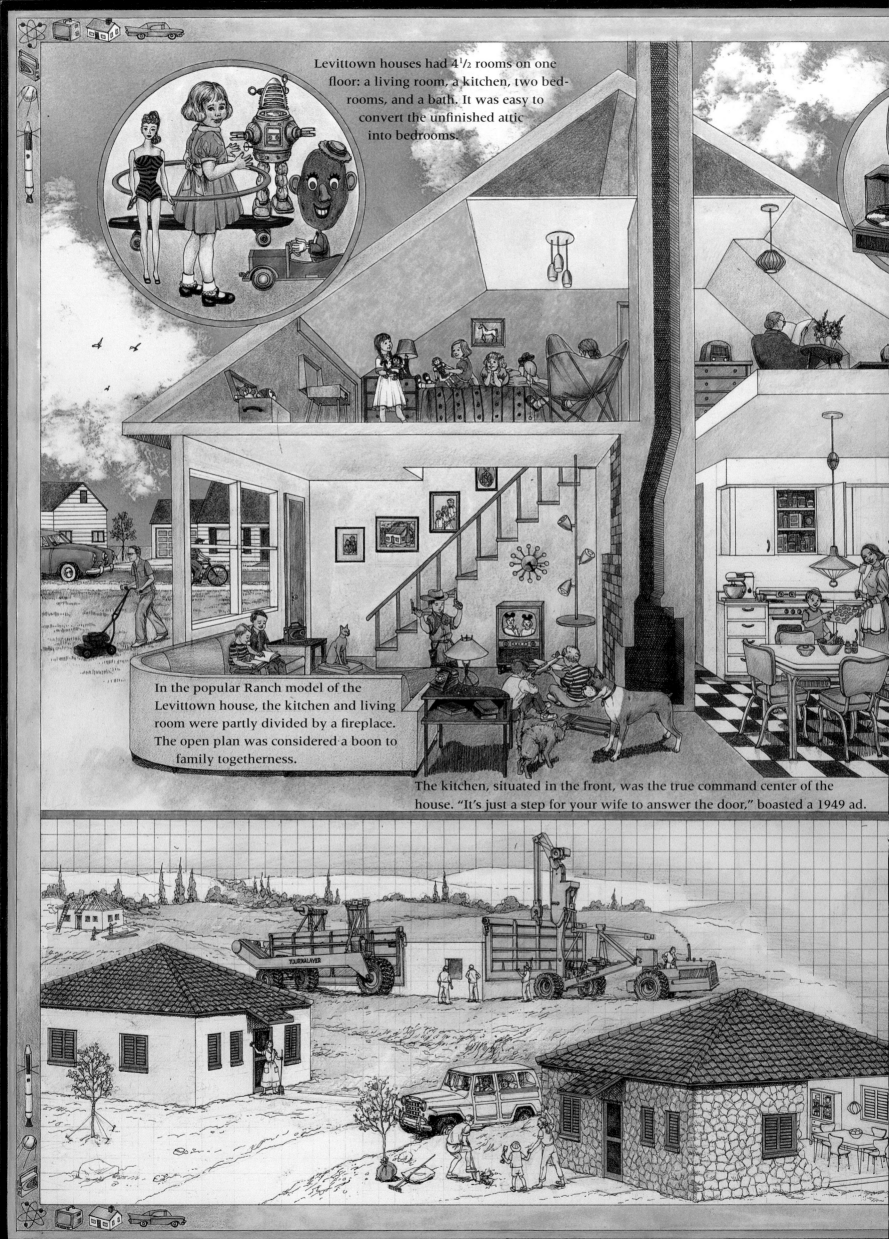

Levittown houses had 4½ rooms on one floor: a living room, a kitchen, two bedrooms, and a bath. It was easy to convert the unfinished attic into bedrooms.

In the popular Ranch model of the Levittown house, the kitchen and living room were partly divided by a fireplace. The open plan was considered a boon to family togetherness.

The kitchen, situated in the front, was the true command center of the house. "It's just a step for your wife to answer the door," boasted a 1949 ad.

'51 Olds

'53 Ford

'56 Chevy

'57 Cadillac

RANCHES FOR ALL

Levittown, Long Island, about twenty-five miles east of New York City, was one of the first post-World War II suburban housing developments in the United States. It was made possible by legislation that put the U.S. government in the business of financing homes for soldiers returning from the war. In 1947, two thousand houses were built and quickly occupied by veterans and their families. Thousands more were soon to come. By 1951, the U.S. Census Bureau was ready to declare that the "average" American lived in Levittown: he was male, thirty years old, had a wife and two children, and owned a refrigerator, a radio, and a telephone.

The building of so many houses that were virtually identical gave rise to a chorus of criticism over "cookie-cutter" homes with "cookie-cutter" families, but both the builders and tenants of Levittown took pride in the amenities that mass-production made possible. These were snug, comfortable houses with affordable appliances that made the daily round of household chores less arduous. Soon, owners were customizing their homes, and today no one of the original houses looks like any other one.

A Jewish family in Israel lights Hanukkah candles. In the United States and Israel, rising birth rates generated an enormous demand for single-family houses in the 1950s.

Settling In   After World War II, builders pioneered mass-production techniques for constructing houses. The founding of the State of Israel in 1948, for example, led to an immediate need for housing for hundreds of thousands of immigrants. Before the year was out, the existing housing stock was exhausted. Many immigrants joined *moshavim*, rural settlements built on land leased from the government. The typical *moshav* is a cooperative, an economic unit using as little hired labor as possible whose members buy and sell goods collectively.

Houses in the *moshavim* were constructed quickly and cheaply. Unlike the wood-frame Levittown houses, many had walls of poured concrete. At left, a mobile steel mold called a tournalayer is being used to make a shell. A typical *moshav* house was a bit smaller than a Levittown Ranch, with a kitchen, bathroom, and two bedrooms, but no living room. It wasn't until the 1960s and 1970s that many families were able to add additional rooms to their houses.

OUTER SPACE

The building of dwellings where human life is not sustainable—such as outer space and the bottom of the ocean—poses technological obstacles that are only now beginning to be solved. In space, there is no air and no water and no source of food. On a space station the necessities of life are obtained via recycling (oxygen from the carbon dioxide breathed out by its occupants, water from urine) or supply ships from Earth. The station itself is hermetically sealed against the deadly vacuum of space, and life-support systems would fail without the energy that is collected by the delicate solar arrays. On board, the fans that circulate the air are so loud that some astronauts return from missions with their hearing impaired.

In conditions of zero gravity, most people become disoriented, so space-station interiors are outfitted with a "floor" and "walls" and "ceiling," although in reality there is no up and down. Once lost, even the smallest objects can wreak havoc as they float through the cabin, and simple tasks like washing up require complex devices. Up to now, the longest that a human being has lived in these demanding conditions is 438 days, a record held by Valeri Poliakov aboard the Russian Mir space station, pictured here.

The first inhabitants of a space station were three Russian cosmonauts who spent twenty-three days aboard Salyut in June 1971. They were killed attempting to return to Earth. Over the next two decades, the Russians developed techniques to maintain space stations using both manned and unmanned supply vessels, and in 1995 the United States and Russia began joint missions aboard Russia's Mir space station, which was adapted so that the U.S. space shuttle could dock on it. Mir consists of seven modules—the oldest, the Core Module, dates back to 1986—that were launched separately and assembled in space.

Inner Space

Our first "house" is very much like a space station: up until some time in the seventh month after we are conceived, we are as vulnerable to the world outside the womb as the astronaut is to the airless universe beyond the thin walls of the space station.

Perhaps the first drawing of a child in the womb (left) was made by Leonardo da Vinci (1452–1519) in about 1512, in a notebook devoted to embryology. Leonardo clearly grasped the significance of the umbilical cord and the complex membranes of the sac that holds the fetus (as the human embryo after about the twelfth week of gestation is called), and he probably guessed correctly that both of these features play a vital role in sustaining life before birth.

We use the expression "to go back to the womb" to suggest a desire to retreat from the pressures of the world. As protected as it is, however, the fetus in the womb is part of the world at large, and through the womb's organs come oxygen and nutrients, as well as sensations of sound and movement that convey information about the outside environment. All effective human shelters, all "houses," balance enclosure and openness to different degrees. Today, to be at home in the universe beyond the Earth's atmosphere requires a kind of mechanical womb. Who knows what kinds of intergalactic houses the future will bring.

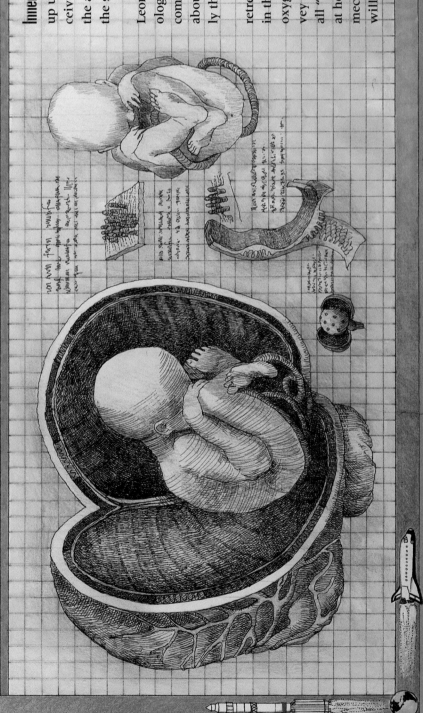

FUNCTIONAL DWELLINGS

If it does nothing else, any structure for living must provide shelter from the elements. When the men on Ernest Shackelton's stranded Antarctic expedition used an upturned boat as a temporary house and survived inside it for many months (right), they were being pragmatic. Very few dwellings, however, are as narrowly practical as this one was. Virtually every human habitation reflects some cultural ideal. An amusing metaphor for this process would be the Swiss Family Robinson Treehouse at Disneyland. Supposedly a shipwrecked family's improvised shelter, this is in reality a complex combination of domestic and nautical architecture embellished with rustic motifs—what one expert wryly calls Castaway Style.

An unusual variation on the house as a simple shelter is the raft, named *Kon-Tiki,* that Thor Heyerdahl built to prove his thesis that Polynesia was settled by oceangoing peoples from South America (left). It is impossible to say, of course, whether Heyerdahl's theory was correct, because any traces of such rafts would have vanished hundreds of years ago. There's something persuasive, however, in the fact that he built the simplest craft possible—a wooden platform with a single sail and a shed on it—and succeeded in reaching land thousands of miles away on his first try. What is so striking about this experience, in direct contrast to Shackleton's, is how benign nature can be. The raft was carried along day after mild day in the Humboldt Current, and dinner, in the form of flying fish, literally leapt out of the sea onto the deck. In such idyllic conditions, why bother with anything more complicated than a roof to screen out the sun and deflect the warm rain?

At the opposite end of the scale from *Kon-Tiki* are shelters constructed to protect their inhabitants from the worst damage that nature or humanity can inflict—for example, fall-out shelters, storm cellars, and bunkers. Around the world, castles and fortresses bear witness to the enormous importance of fortified houses in the past. Even Leonardo da Vinci spent considerable time devising fortifications for his various patrons. As recently as World War I, armies dug substantial trenches deep into the ground to withstand month after month of intense artillery bombardment (right). It is difficult to conceive of a more miserable fate than to be condemned to spend days in the cold and damp, listening for the nerve-racking buzz of incoming shells. Historically, every structure built to withstand a man-made or natural disaster has proved vulnerable in the long run.

The most remarkable class of structures for living consists of self-contained worlds that hurtle through space, carrying sufficient provisions to support their crews for months and even years at a time. None of these are land-based, although science-fiction writers occasionally imagine such juggernauts on distant planets—the spice factories of Frank Herbert's *Dune* are an example. Until very recently, only oceangoing ships fitted this description. We are perhaps on the brink of an era of manned outposts in space and undersea as well. All of these "machines for living" have in common a high degree of technical sophistication. A whaling ship (top left) is relatively small, yet it contains numerous complex operating systems that must all function efficiently: hunting; processing (of whale bone and oil); navigation; maintainance; what might be called "life support" (food supplies and preparation); and finally administration (for organizing work and maintaining discipline). A space station (bottom left) is not appreciably different, although it carries a far smaller crew and proportionately more of its systems are devoted to life support. Like the rest of the "houses" on this page, the whaling ship and the space station use little of their precious space for non-utilitarian purposes, although both contain elements that are expressive of the cultural and aesthetic ideals of their builders.

THE HOUSE AND SOCIETY

Today, in Europe and the United States, the ordinary house is a bastion of the family, and its members venture forth either together or individually to participate in the institutions of the larger society. Private and public realms are clearly separated, with different values and standards of behavior. In some cultures, however, the house and its organization mirror that of the society. For example, the Iroquois thought of the longhouse (left) as a microcosm of their political community. Just as the many disparate family members were expected to compromise their individual interests for the good of the group, so were the tribes of the confederation to do the same on a larger scale. In fact, the physical arrangement of the longhouse afforded its inhabitants very little privacy at all. Since it would have been a simple matter to build interior walls within the structure, this was clearly a choice based on deeply held cultural ideals.

One of the few classes of persons whose privacy is not respected in the West is political leaders. This long predates the rise of democratic institutions. In fact, from the Middle Ages to the French Revolution, a monarch's life was intensely public, and virtually every domestic ritual was an occasion for public ceremony. The "house" itself—be it palace, such as Hampton Court (right), or castle—was a symbol of the wealth and power of the realm, and much of the artwork and decoration within it was designed to reinforce this purpose. A powerful king or queen would not be embarrassed by the public disclosure of his or her private behavior, and actions that are looked upon with censure today, such as the taking of a mistress or a lover, would usually be scrutinized in terms of their impact on shifting alliances within the court rather than their moral implications. A monarch tired of the public arena might have a private apartment, but could not dispense with a set of public "private" rooms as well.

When people live in groups, they submit to a set of rules governing behavior. A mild example would be a college dormitory segregated by gender that does not permit visits by people of the opposite sex after a certain hour. Many institutions whose members live together communally are far more strict. When people choose to live communally as a matter of religious conviction—as in monasteries (above) and convents—they make rules that have strong spiritual and moral intent. Daily schedules are made for everyone, for example, with plenty of time devoted to worship. Members may be required to take vows that shape their lives in dramatic ways, such as a commitment to poverty or chastity. In the army, new recruits are gathered into separate barracks where they are expected to adhere to rigorous regulations regarding seemingly trivial points of housekeeping. The underlying purpose of these rules is to rapidly transform a miscellaneous collection of individuals into a group with a strong sense of collective identity and discipline. This regimen may be an ordeal for many, but it tends to work.

Some collective living arrangements are far from voluntary. The fact is that, for better or worse, there are people everywhere who are unmanageable. The treatment of these people raises some of the thorniest moral issues that a society has to deal with. At one extreme there are criminals who must be confined because they are an obvious danger to others. Very few moralists would argue that murderers, for example, should be permitted to roam at will, and we tend not to be terribly concerned about how they are treated in prison. The problem is that throughout history and around the world, many people are incarcerated for reasons that are not so cut-and-dried as commiting murder and other crimes. These "reasons" can range from the simple fact of racial or ethnic identity to the holding of political or religious opinions abhorrent to those in power. We often make heroes out of people who endured or even escaped imprisonment in the past, if changing attitudes about justice have made them look more like victims than criminals in retrospect. In prisons (right), unlike, say, colleges, rules are by definition imposed on unwilling inmates. Many prisoners undoubtedly adjust to prison life to the point where they cannot imagine another home. This is not what we planned when we put them away.

THE FORMS OF HOUSES

The world's cultures have produced many different architectures. Each one has its own logic, dictated by available materials and manpower, technological sophistication, and aesthetic values. Domed houses, such as the igloo of the Eskimo (far left) and the woven hut of the Zulu (left), are both aesthetically pleasing and structurally very strong. They can be easily constructed with flexible tree branches or out of mud, clay, or snow, but tend to be small, with only one room. The larger they are, the more difficult they are to build.

There are thousands of types of wooden houses. One of the simplest is the log cabin, found in both Russia (right) and the United States where there are extensive virgin forests. (It takes a lot of mature trees to make one log cabin.) The beauty of the log cabin is that it doesn't require a frame. It's built from the ground up, as one log is placed atop another. The logs dovetail at the corners, ensuring the stability of the structure. Usually, mud or plaster is pressed between the logs to make the house weatherproof.

The most common type of wood construction for small houses uses a system of beams to frame the structure. These beams are then enclosed, usually with plywood or bricks. In half-timber construction (left), you can see the building frame because it hasn't been fully covered over. Most small buildings around the world aren't designed by professional architects. Instead, vernacular styles are passed down from one generation of local builders to the next, gradually changing as new techniques are hesitantly tried. In Northern Europe, for example, the design of half-timbered buildings varies by region, and it's easy to learn to distinguish where one is from the houses one sees.

Before the Industrial Revolution, an architect was usually called in when a building had a special purpose or was being commissioned by someone with wealth, status, or power. Generally speaking, only palaces and the homes of aristocrats were designed by architects, who in turn could call upon highly skilled craftspeople to create extraordinary ensembles combining many different decorative arts and often using rare and costly materials. History has preserved the names of all of the architects and artists who designed Versailles (above), and many of the workmen who executed their plans are remembered as well.

As construction has become more complex and technical in modern times, architects and engineers are needed for a greater variety of buildings. (Far more multistory apartment buildings than small single-family houses are professionally designed.) In industrial societies, both the state and real-estate developers commission housing, often hiring distinguished architects.

The greatest architects are inventors of new forms—they may begin with vernacular ideas, such as a decorative motif particular to the region where they live, but they will use them in a new way. For example, Antoní Gaudí adapted elements of Spanish medieval architecture in his designs (left), but no one would confuse one of his creations with a medieval building—it looks original.

THE SINGLE-FAMILY HOUSE

It is probably the case that throughout history, most of the world's families have lived in small houses with one or two rooms that did not have distinct functions. The same space is used for eating and sleeping, working and playing, by family members of both sexes and all ages. This medieval peasants' cottage (left) is a good example, but so would be the longhouse of the Iroquois. In such houses, furnishings and utensils are also likely to be relatively undifferentiated and simple. For centuries, for example, people in the West sat upon stools without backs or arms. Not even the wealthy used chairs, although a king or queen might have a throne.

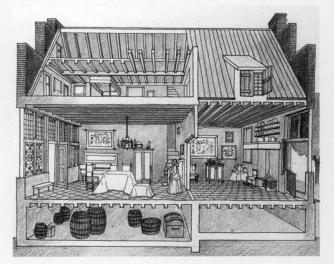

The evolution of the single-family house as we know it is largely the story of two separate strands of development. The first involved the differentiation of rooms by function. The second saw an increasing emphasis on the physical comfort of the inhabitants.

Probably the first room to be separated from the rest of the house was the kitchen, which was moved to the back, where it remained (as in the seventeenth-century Puritan house above) until quite recently. The seventeenth-century Dutch were the first to build single-family houses (right) that provided both comfort and the familiar domestic feeling that can come only when rooms have different functions. It's interesting to note that these houses came about not so much because new technology was available as because people had new aspirations.

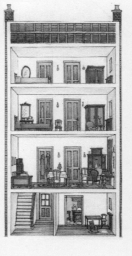

It took hundreds of years for technology and industry to fill these new rooms with familiar appliances and furnishings. In Europe, upholstered furniture, for example (far left), was first produced for the very wealthy—in the eighteenth century—and was made affordable to the middle classes only at the end of the nineteenth. Functional bathrooms (left) had to wait for the widespread availability of indoor plumbing, something that can be provided only through complex social and technological planning.

The population explosion and technological advances of the Industrial Revolution made it both possible and necessary to build multiple-family dwellings in cities. London, with its thousands of modestly proportioned town houses (right), was the pacesetter for innovations in housing in the nineteenth century. Gas lighting, coal heating, indoor plumbing—all had their first grand tryout there. Many of the familiar sentiments of Victorian literature—the cozy domesticity of warm rooms with soft illumination, for example—can be traced to these novel amenities.

Sometime late in the century, New York took over as the city that set the tone for developments in residential housing, but this was largely a question of scale. In the land of the elevator, buildings went higher and higher, although in truth, the typical New York apartment of the twentieth century (far right) was not so different from the London flat of one hundred years earlier—except for the fact that many of the housekeeping chores once performed by hand were now mechanized. This was made possible by electricity, which not only powered the subways under the streets but spawned a seemingly inexhaustible number of laborsaving and life-enhancing devices, from the electric light and the telephone to the washing machine and the TV—all things, by the way, that are perfectly adaptable to the houses that the Dutch built four hundred years ago, as many in Holland have happily discovered.

ACKNOWLEDGMENTS

I would like to thank the following members of my studio for their invaluable assistance in the production of this book: Kirsten Lorenz, Neil Mahimtura, David Mak, PoShan Lee, Jackie Ling, Wendy Kui, Dickson Leung, Christopher Zaccone, Ryan Kasal, and Maureen Lorenz.

Special thanks are due to my editor and friend, Eric Himmel, whose great patience and creative assistance helped make this project a reality.

Thanks again to the special skills of Darilyn Lowe Carnes for the design of this book.

Finally and always, thanks to my wife, Maureen, and my daughters, Margaret and Kirsten, for always being true.

Albert Lorenz

EDITOR: Eric Himmel
DESIGNER: Darilyn Lowe Carnes

Library of Congress Cataloging-in-Publication Data
Lorenz, Albert, 1941–
    House : showing how people have lived throughout history with examples drawn from the lives of legendary men and women / by Albert Lorenz, with Joy Schleh.
       p.   cm.
    ISBN 0–8109–1196–5
    1. Dwellings—History.   I. Schleh, Joy.   II. Title.
GT170.L68   1998
    307.3'36'09—DC21   98–26412

Printed and bound in China

Harry N. Abrams, Inc.
100 Fifth Avenue
New York, N.Y. 10011
www.abramsbooks.com